Cryptocurrency

Cryptocurrency, Volume 1

Tim Mathis

Published by Brendan Gallagher, 2018.

While every precaution has been taken in the preparation of this book, the publisher assumes no responsibility for errors or omissions, or for damages resulting from the use of the information contained herein.

CRYPTOCURRENCY

First edition. January 11, 2018.

Copyright © 2018 Tim Mathis.

ISBN: 979-8215300879

Written by Tim Mathis.

Table of Contents

CRYPTOCURRENCY:

The world of cryptocurrency

Introduction

Chances are if you're reading this book, you've already heard something about Cryptocurrency and it has definitely peaked your interest. You're probably thinking you'd like to get in on the profits that are beckoning you, but don't know where to start.

Well, you've come to the right place.

Many people believe that cryptocurrency will eventually replace our current economic system. That's a rather bold declaration considering that the system we are using now has been in place for hundreds of years. However, if you've learned anything about economic history, no matter where you come from, whose culture you adopt, or your status in life, the economic and political fabric of the world is never completely set. It is perpetually in a state of flux, and when the systems in place no longer meet the needs of the public, they must change. We are on the precipice of change right now with cryptocurrency.

Ask one hundred people if they know what cryptocurrency is, and you'll probably find that only half of them have ever heard of it, likely half of them have no idea what it is, and the odds are that half of those who do know what it is, have any detailed knowledge. And likely only a small percentage of them actually have earned or invested any money in it.

So, how is it that people are touting this as the next big thing in economic evolution? The answer is simple. While the percentage of individuals with an understanding of it is yet small, the knowledge of this fantastic innovative moment in economic growth is growing.

It's expanding, as cryptocurrency has already been demonstrated to be the ideal solution for numerous people who are grappling with this unrelenting and slanted financial environment. The chances are countless, and all it needs is a brief know-how, and then you can begin creating your new economic portfolio using cryptocurrency and get spruce earnings in the process.

Thanks for downloading this book. It's my firm belief that it will provide you with all the answers to your questions

Chapter 1: What Is Cryptocurrency?

Every society since mankind began trading things of value had some type of currency. Notice, I used the word currency, not money. The reason for this is because money is merely one form of currency; it is used to transfer VALUE from one party to the next. Now that we are in the digital age, cryptocurrency is simply currency in digital form.

In the past, individuals used all sorts of things to transfer value from one person to the next. At one point, they were using livestock (cattle, goats, sheep, pigs, chickens, etc.). Later, when carrying around a few cows every time you needed to go shopping turned out to be cumbersome, they began trading shells (conch, puka, etc.) or beads, after that it was bone, metal, and now, paper (actually paper money is not really paper at all, it's a secret blend of bamboo and cotton fibers, woven together with silk threads).

But I'm sure you've noticed over the past few years, that the need to carry around physical money is not as important or necessary as it once was. People now do much of their buying and selling either online or with credit or debit cards.

Eventually, physical money may completely fade from use. What's now taking its place is cryptocurrency, the next step up in a digital form of currency that is traded and managed entirely online.

The term cryptocurrency is a combination of two Greek terms, with the key being "crypto," meaning "to be kept hidden." In English, we adopt this as a source word very regularly. Initially, a crypt is a site where you can isolate dead bodies, also, cryptic means to have a secret or hidden persona, cryptography, on the other hand, means the art of cracking codes to get their hidden intent or the manner of determining them.

This is the solid concept behind cryptocurrency; the design of (encrypt) writing code or (decrypt) decoding.

It is the application of a compound code to encrypt a data alteration to exchange value. This is always done by forming complicated mathematical theorems and sole protocols created to secure the codes and make them practically impossible to duplicate, break, or counterfeit. These customs not only shield the transaction between the two parties involved, but they also hide the names of all those connected.

The beauty of cryptocurrency is that it is not under the control of any governmental agency, so there is no centralized institution or political entity responsible for determining its value. The value, therefore, is determined primarily by its users and is based on supply and demand. This causes the price to fluctuate more like that of stocks and bonds.

It is used just like you would use a physical currency; you can make purchases, save it, trade it, or even invest it in the same manner. The difference is that you would never hold them in your hands; they only exist as lines of code maintained in a database, and just like with physical currency, you cannot change its value. If you have $20 bill in your hand, there is no way you can change that to $100 or any other value. It is what it is. However, you can always add to it, subtract from it, or save it anytime you like.

History of Cryptocurrency

Cryptocurrency, like all other innovations, was created to solve a particular problem. In the beginning, it was never meant to become the preferred currency of trade, but was to be used as a side product to complement an already existing digital currency system.

However, with the introduction of cryptocurrency, people could use digital currency without going through a centralized server without any specialized regulation, or a single authority overseeing everything for the first time. The system was based entirely on P2P (person to person) networks used as an assurance against double spending.

While it may not have been the original intent of this new monetary instrument, another issue that cryptocurrency resolved was creating a system that eliminated the need for a third-party to be involved in transactions. This automatically provided a more secure system for making online payments. It also eliminated the cost of having to pay exorbitant fees for every transaction made. The new digital currency was designed to be completely independent of any central regulation or third-party involvement.

Actually, the original intent for cryptocurrency was as a wealth enrichment tool. As there is a cap on the amount of cryptocurrency available on the market, the more people use it, the higher the demand. Therefore, over time, the value of the currency will gradually increase.

With this system, all transactions take place between the two parties involved and not any other third parties. No transaction takes place unless there is an absolute consensus and no funds can be transferred unless it is legitimate.

What Makes Cryptocurrency Different from Normal Currency?

There is not much difference between cryptocurrency and our traditional currency when it comes to spending. You can use them to purchase anything you can purchase with regular currency as long as the other party is willing to trade with them.

With more than 1000 cryptocurrencies available to choose from and more coming, there's a pretty good bet that no matter what type of business you want to conduct you will be able to trade using some form of cryptocurrency. The biggest and probably the most well-known among them is the Bitcoin, but we'll talk more about that in the next chapter.

Quite often, you will hear them referred to as coins: Bitcoin, Dogecoin, Litecoin, etc. but the word is used only as a point of reference. Cryptocurrency does not have a physical form. Still, there are some similarities, but the differences make them unique.

Chapter 2: The Most Common Cryptocurrencies

A s more and more places of business are in a position to accept a digital currency as payment for their product or services, cryptocurrencies will gradually begin to overtake physical money. But unless you're dealing with them on a regular basis, you're probably not aware of how many different cryptocurrencies are already floating around the market.

One of the unique advantages of cryptocurrency is that they are created to fulfill a void in the economy. Unlike traditional dollars and coins, a cryptocurrency can be designed to achieve a certain purpose. Of course, not all cryptocurrencies are the same. Because they are so easy to create, some have been developed as a joke, others for scams, and still others for special events or occasions.

However, there are plenty of solid digital currencies to choose from depending on your needs. There is no doubt that you will find the perfect one for you. Below we will take a closer look at some of the most common currencies available and see why they are so important.

Bitcoin

Most likely when you think of digital currency, Bitcoin is the name that comes to your mind. Just like the name Xerox is almost synonymous with copy, Bitcoin is often confused and believed to be the only cryptocurrency around.

Some people actually refer to it as the "people's currency" because they expect it to be the one cryptocurrency that will uproot and replace all national currencies in the future.

A mysteriously anonymous figure, Satoshi Nakamoto, created Bitcoin. It was the very first digital currency of its kind. It holds the largest market cap to date, placing it well over any other currency on the list.

For those interested in investing in cryptocurrencies, the best place to start is with Bitcoin. It is without a doubt the leader of the pack and has had the longest history of all the coins on the market. As a matter of fact, all other coins are referred to as altcoins (alternative coins) because they are viewed as alternatives to Bitcoin.

People use them to buy or sell and even to pay for services both on and offline. It is even possible now to pick up Bitcoins through ATMs being introduced in some countries.

While it does require the use of codes to buy or sell Bitcoins, it is not necessary to understand all the technical details to get the benefits they offer.

Ethereum (Ether)

Like Bitcoin, Ethereum is a public Blockchain digital currency with a few technical differences. Where Bitcoin is geared more towards keeping track of who owns the currency, Ethereum is designed more towards the function of the programming code.

Ethereum is most known for its use of Smart Contracts, offering people the ability to code and enact very definite contract terms without the involvement of a third-party. At its basic level, it solves the problem of handling legal contracts online. When a smart contract is put into motion, it works like a self-operating computer program designed to take action automatically once agreed upon conditions are met. Whatever the system is programmed to do, it will follow those procedures exactly. There is no possibility to censor or interfere with the parameters set.

Another unique feature of Ethereum is that there are very few limitations on Ethereum's ability to process code. A developer is free to come up with thousands of different applications, so its potential is virtually endless.

This currency has been divided into two distinct forms: Ethereum (ETH) and Ethereum Classic (ETC). Created in 2015 by Vitalik Buterin, it has already reached a market cap of more than $1 billion.

Ripple

Not only is Ripple a digital currency, it is also an open payment network where users can transfer currency from one party to the next. It is designed to work pretty much the same way that Bitcoin does on a decentralized network using the same format that the Internet does with the information.

Its purpose is to make a connection between different payment systems used by different parties. It eliminates the snags for different companies using different systems, so that transfer of funds is practically seamless regardless of the country it is going to.

Not only will it give users the ability to connect with users of other forms of digital currency, but it will also speed up the transfer process and provide more stability. With Ripple, there is no need to wait for confirmation, so every transaction goes through quickly.

Monero

One of the biggest problems people deal with on online technology is that of maintaining privacy, which is Monero's primary concern. While this may present a problem in most western governments, Monero is extremely important in nations where one's identity must be protected at all costs. For example, in the USA, when people are concerned about their identity, it is about protecting their assets. They don't want someone to come in and steal the value they have accumulated. However, for someone who lives in places where playing on the economic playground could be perceived as anti-government, secrecy could mean your life.

In addition to being private, it is secure, and anything traded through Monero is untraceable. It uses its own unique cryptography that ensures that every transaction made cannot be linked to the parties involved. This is accomplished through the use of multiple keys. Unlike other cryptocurrencies where the user may have one public view key and one private view key, with Monero your public key is provided to generate a one-time public address. The private key, however, is given to the receiver to scan the Blockchain to search for the funds they are to receive.

But you will also have a public spend key and a private spend key, which have their own unique functions they are to perform.

One of the reasons Monero is so popular is because you can maintain total control over all of your transactions. Therefore, you and only you are responsible for what happens to your money.

Litecoin

Litecoin is very similar to Bitcoin when it comes to code, but there are a few significant functional differences.

While both currencies have the same purpose, Litecoin processes much faster than Bitcoin. Since Bitcoin transactions are not complete until they have received confirmation, users must "wait" for "miners" to verify every transaction. This process could take as little as 10 minutes, but it could also take much longer. Litecoin does the same thing in an even shorter time frame.

Like Bitcoin, it is a peer-to-peer currency that provides immediate payments to anyplace in the world for a minuscule fee. The same powerful mathematical equations used to provide the network's security also gives each user the ability to manage their own finances.

Litecoin uses what is called an Open Source Protocol, which lets developers know where to access the user's source code.

Golem

The Golem Network has been compared to the Airbnb for computers, allowing its users to rent out their computing power to other users online. It allows other machines located in different places around the globe to transact and work together on a particular project.

Golem also takes advantage of the same smart contracts capabilities that Ethereum uses. However, as Ethereum allows the user to buy fuel, cars, and pay their owners, Golem does the same thing with computer power.

Through Golem, users help to create the world's largest supercomputer, an interplanetary network comprised of everything from personal laptops in people's homes to entire data centers; all completely decentralized, meaning no one is monitoring its works.

This network would not be owned, managed, or operated by any individual, government, or corporation and it cannot be utilized to monopolize the economy or regulate people's abilities to control their own money, and it can never be shut down.

When your computer joins the Golem system, it could be used to perform scientific research, render graphics, create Artificial Intelligence, analyze data, or mine for a cryptocurrency.

Factom

One of the things that Factom is known for is its ability to solve many business challenges because of how it maintains unalterable records.

It creates a layer of data using the Bitcoin Blockchain as its foundation. Their distributed ledger technology can maintain millions of records on a Blockchain with just one hash.

Businesses, as well as governments, can both use Factom as a means of documenting their data in a way that prevents it from being altered, deleted, or backdated in any way. This assures that all data stored remains intact and ensures user privacy at the same time.

Because this information is stored on a decentralized network, the threat of hackers or organizations and their attempts to tamper or interfere with its processes is virtually impossible.

Through Factom, users can store all kinds of data, making it perfect for all sorts of applications. Medical records, supply chain management, legal applications, and more can make use of this type of cryptocurrency.

As we said before, there are now more than a thousand cryptocurrencies to choose from, and more are being created regularly. When it comes to investing or doing business with these currencies, it's important that you learn as much as you can about each one.

It can be really exciting to think about the potential each of these has, but you must proceed with caution. While there are many available, you need to know that the currency you choose has the opportunity to bring you the results you seek. This requires that you ask the right questions.

It is not enough that the currency you choose can be used to purchase or sell a product. If you want to make money using cryptocurrency, it also has to be appealing to the masses. Remember, the value of any currency is not backed up by any government or organization, but is determined by the basics of supply and demand. For that to happen, it must solve a particular problem.

You'll notice that all the currencies listed above address a unique problem.

However, some digital currencies solve problems, but not the problems that many people must deal with. It means that only a few will see a need to trade with those currencies, thus limiting your profit potential.

Whatever problem these currencies address, it must be something you understand. Take the time to learn about the technology behind it, learn about its developers and the team who put it together. It can also be beneficial if you can visualize where that currency will go in the future and see yourself as part of its ultimate goal.

Also, it is important to know which merchants you might expect to accept that currency and decide if you are likely to be dealing with that type of business. Once you've learned and understood all of these things, your first decision in investing in cryptocurrency is made. You are ready for the next step.

Chapter 3: Understanding Blockchain Technology

To keep things simple, Blockchain can often be considered as a database. There are some similarities as the Blockchain is going to store transactions as well as other records of value. However, it is not enough to say that Blockchain is just a new database type. Yes, when you are working with a Blockchain ledger, it will store information, but saying that it is just a database is not going to be enough to explain some of the neat things that this technology can do or the reasons that Bitcoin and other industries are applying this technology.

The best way to see how the Blockchain works is to compare it with traditional databases. With these, when you put a new transaction on the ledger, you would have to work with a third party that you trusted, like a financial institution or a government, to help record the information and keep it all safe for you. It was the responsibility of these third parties to help build up trust between themselves and their customers. For example, a bank can build up this trust because it has the government behind it, ensuring the money, so you will always be able to get your money back out no matter what kind of trouble the bank runs into.

This trust is really important when we complete our transactions. Any time that we do a transfer of money, such as when we make payments for goods and services, we have to trust the bank or financial institution that we work with. They will take the exact right amount out of our accounts and then give it to the right seller. The seller also has to trust this system as well, trusting that the money will end up in their account and not get lost or be in the wrong amount.

Over the years, we have learned how to trust credit card companies and banks to do these transactions accurately for us, no matter what seller or store we are working with. We also trust that the company will maintain a database that will maintain all of the transactions and that the company will make sure that they keep all of your personal information safe from hackers and other individuals. We know that when we go onto our accounts, we will be able to see the right amount of money there because the financial institution has shown they can be trustworthy.

When it comes to using the Blockchain technology, you will be able to get this trust and the same security without needing to rely on those third parties in the process. This is why Blockchain is used in Bitcoin and other digital currencies.

These currencies are still growing and haven't had the time to build up the trust that is needed, so Blockchain helps to add in the trust. These currencies have no government backing, are brand new, and just haven't had the history to see how well they would do. This means that Blockchain has some work ahead of it, but it is possible to rely on this technology to complete your transactions.

CRYPTOCURRENCY

As the database for Blockchain is decentralized, it makes it easier for the user to put trust in a system that doesn't have a government or bank behind it.

Anyone who is on the Blockchain network will be able to view and check on all their transactions, which will make it easier to create transparency and some trust in the network.

This is why right now, the most common reason for people to use Blockchain ledgers is with Bitcoin and some of the other cryptocurrencies. This technology allows users to complete transactions with each other in just a few minutes while still keeping their information safe. However, there are a few other methods and applications for how you can use the Blockchain technology. The Blockchain can handle any valuable information, so any industry that will handle property, shares, money, or digital files will be able to benefit from this technology.

How Does Blockchain Technology Work?

So, now that we have spent some time talking about Blockchain and some of the benefits that come with this technology, it is time to understand how this type of technology is going to work. It is pretty simple for users to use it as it only takes a few minutes to do the transactions and you are signed up automatically when you join a digital currency. But the things that happen behind the scenes are a bit more complex, which helps to provide the trust and security that the system needs.

Since we will mostly associate Blockchain with Bitcoin and some of the other digital currencies that are out there, it is the easiest to take a look at how Blockchain will work on these networks. It will work similarly on other networks as well, but this will help to keep things in order. On the Blockchain, when you complete a transaction it will show up, in order, on one of the blocks you are using. When the block is filled up, it will join in the permanent record and will link together with the other blocks that you have completed to form a chain. This all works together to help keep your information in order and keeps it secure from others who may want to take a look at the information.

Each block in the Blockchain is going to be responsible for holding onto all the important information about the transactions that you complete and each of the blocks will hold onto a lot of data. Depending on the network that you work with, these blocks could contain information about currencies, digital rights, identity, and property titles to name a few. Since these blocks can hold onto so much information and will keep that information safe, Blockchain is one of the best ways to help people interact, send money, and even make their purchases.

When you decide to join the Bitcoin network, and you create your own Bitcoin address, you will join in its Blockchain. Each user will receive a block that they will be able to fill up each time that they finish a new transaction. These blocks can hold onto quite a bit of information and some people will fill them up quickly, and others may take a bit longer.

After the block has filled up with the different transactions that you are working on, they are going to become a part of the permanent record on Bitcoin. They will join the Bitcoin network's Blockchain, and you will start making your own personal Blockchain, which will contain all of the blocks that contain your own transactions.

When one block is all filled up, it is time to receive another block, which the system will send over to you automatically. You can then start to fill up that block with transactions as well, and the process keeps going for as long as you keep using the network. Every user on the Bitcoin network, or whatever platform you are using at the time, will have their own Blockchain that is full of personal transactions. But as the blocks fill up, those will be added to the permanent Blockchain that the Bitcoin network relies on so the information is kept safe. This process works together to make sure that the Bitcoin network remains transparent to use.

This can all seem a little bit confusing right now, but one way to think about how Blockchain works is to think of it as your own bank statement. Each block that you receive will be a monthly statement that you get from the bank. You can look it over to see what transactions you have completed in recent times and check to make sure it is all good. After you have finished a few of these statements, they will all become part of your bank history. They will be a part of your permanent record with the bank (or regarding the Blockchain, with the Bitcoin network), and you can always look back to see what payments you made, what funds you received, and any other transaction.

The main difference between these is that Blockchain is going to be online and will only be in charge of things that happen on the Bitcoin network.

One nice thing that comes with the Blockchain technology is that it works with Bitcoin in order to keep your transactions safe and secure. There are some special codes or some hashes that will be added in so that hackers and other people won't be able to steal your information. Anyone who is on the network can see these transactions, but they will have to look through these special hashes to see what is going on. It is the work of the miners on the Bitcoin network that will make sure the Blockchain ledger is secure, and they will be rewarded with 25 Bitcoin each time that they are successful.

The job of the miner may sound easy, but some complications can come with it, and they are in charge of maintaining most of the security of this system. They will need to come up with the unique hashes that will help to hide all of your information so that it will be safe from others who want to look. But they can't just go through and write out any random number that they would like, or anyone could do this, and all of the coins on Bitcoin would be mined.

Instead, there are a few rules to the hashes that are created. First, the beginning of each hash needs to have a certain number of zeroes, and since you don't know how a hash will look until you are done, you could create quite a few of these before getting results. Also, the hashes have to be designed so that if any one character in the chain is changed, it is going to change up all of the characters that come after it as well. This makes it complicated to make a good hash, but it does make it easier to catch if someone has been messing around with the Blockchain.

As you can guess, the process of creating one of these codes is not the easiest, but these rules ensure that your information is going to stay safe and that not just anyone could add in a random code to the mix. If they could do that, then a code could do the work, and the security would be gone. Right now, the miners will be rewarded with 25 Bitcoin when they are done.

Since a Bitcoin is worth about $3200 right now, this can be a good reward for the work that they are doing. This becomes a win-win situation for everyone who is involved. The miners will get paid well for the work that they are doing, and the users of the network can rest assured that their information will stay safe.

The Blockchain is a really neat piece of technology that has so many potential applications for users to enjoy. Right now, it is the leading force that has helped Bitcoin become so popular, but it is sure to change many other aspects of our world in the future. It is such a simple idea, just a ledger to keep track of transactions, but it is so efficient and easy to use that many platforms for different applications are already in use.

Chapter 4: How Does Cryptocurrency Work?

Just like with any traditional currency, you can use cryptocurrency to make purchases both in the store and online. You can also use them as investment tools or as a means of trading or bartering. While digital currency doesn't necessarily have a face value, as in a physical object that you can hold in your hand and carry it from one place to the next, you do have an online version via your "wallet." In essence, your wallet holds the lines of code that connects you to your currency maintained in the database.

Once all the conditions of a transaction are met, the currency can be transferred to the individual or organization for completion. While this explanation may sound a little complicated, there is really very little difference between conducting a transaction in a traditional bank and trading in cryptocurrency. When you put your money into a bank account, there are certain conditions that you must meet to reclaim it. You may be asked to provide identification, a history of past transactions, or give a signature that matches one they have on file.

In this case, the bank serves as the third-party to verify the data they have on file before you can make any changes to your account. With cryptocurrency, however, you eliminate the middleman, and through the use of a code, you are the party responsible for ensuring that all the conditions are met before deciding to transfer the funds.

There are several steps involved in making a cryptocurrency transaction.

1. The transaction is submitted online.

2. The P2P network nodes receive the request.

3. The network then verifies the identity of the requester and the details of the transaction.

4. The miners then verify, accept, or deny the request.

5. If approved, it is logged into the digital database (the Blockchain).

6. The transaction is then added to a list of stored lines of code. (Once entered here, it can never be altered or deleted.)

7. The transaction is then listed as complete.

While there are quite a few steps involved in this type of transaction, it can usually be finalized in just a matter of minutes. The system is quite efficient and very easy to do. Still, let's take a look at what happens in just a little more detail.

Encryption/Decryption

Encryption is simply the tool used to convert the data relating to the transaction into a line of code. This is done to keep all but the interested parties from accessing the information. Just as you have passwords and key codes to get information on your bank account online, your digital currency will do the same but in a little more detail. The user will create two keys that are linked to each other by a mathematical equation. The public key is used to create the code, which is called the encryption and the second key, called the private key, is used to decode or decrypt the code.

When you are ready to make a payment or purchase, you can do so by giving the other party the public key, which gives them access to your virtual wallet. However, for them to collect on your payment, they must also have the private key, which gives them access to the allocated funds.

Decentralized

Cryptocurrency removes the decision-making power from a central location and transfers it to the parties involved. Rather than having all the data maintained on a single server, the information is stored on a network of centric systems that all follow the same basic mathematical rules that have already been agreed upon.

With a decentralized network, no individual or group has a lot of control over what happens to the money. Its value is determined by the people who are actually using the system. Since every person is connected to every other person, there is no centralized point of weakness where it can fail and impact a mass number of members.

Distributed Systems

Closely related to the decentralized network, a distributed system is a network of autonomous computers that are joined together with middleware. They all share the same resources and perform similar functions for users within an integrated network.

These collections of computers work together as one single unit and share the processing power provided by millions of personal computers around the globe.

Those who wish to become a part of this type of network generally must first download and run a small program that kicks on whenever the computer is out of use.

Open Source Code

An open source code is a software program that anyone can inspect, modify, and enhance. It usually comes with a license allowing programmers to adjust the software in a way that may support their needs. To open source code, the software must meet several different criteria:

- Free redistribution of software

Allows the user to sell or give away the software as a part of an aggregate distribution program from other sources. As a condition of the license, they cannot demand a royalty or fee for this distribution.

- Availability of source code

The source code must be made available, and distribution must be allowed along with the compiled form. How to obtain the source code must be well publicized and made available through the Internet for a reasonable cost.

- Integrity of the author's source code

Restrictions on modifying the source code are only allowed if the license permits "patch files" to be distributed when the intent is to modify the program during a build time. It must be stated in the license that the distribution can only come from a modified source code and may require derived works to use a different name from the original software.

- Anti-discrimination policies

Distribution of an open source code cannot discriminate in any way against any person or group.

- No discrimination against any specific field or endeavor

There can also be no discrimination against any type of business or any particular endeavor. Distribution cannot be refused by any group or organization.

- License cannot be limited to any specific product

It cannot be dependent on any program or any specific distribution.

- It cannot be allowed to restrict any other software program

It is not permitted to require any other program also to be open-source or come in any other form.

- It cannot rely on any individual technology or interface

With open source code, there are different types of licenses that allow for programmers to modify their software under certain conditions.

There are several advantages of using open source code:

> - You get a higher quality of results when the source code is continuously being modified. Each time it is passed around, it is tested and modified, improving the code with each phase.

CRYPTOCURRENCY

- It is a great way for programmers to learn and apply new skills to many popular programs.

- Many believe the open source code is more reliable and secure than the proprietary software as problems are more likely to be identified and corrected.

- It is more likely to be available for longer since it is found in the public domain.

- In most cases, it is free to use and modify.

Public Ledgers (Blockchain)

At the very heart of the database is the public ledger. Sometimes referred to as the Blockchain, it is a public recording of every transaction made on the network.

The public ledger maintains a continuous list of "blocks" where each transaction is recorded in linear and chronological order. As each block is added the ledger, each computer connected to the network (node) automatically receives a downloaded copy.

Transaction

A transaction is created when you use an encrypted electronic signature to send any type of digital currency. It is then added to the Blockchain via a public ledger that is sent out to every node in the network.

Node

Any computer that is part of the global network and is using the protocol to allow the nodes to communicate with each other is a node. Each node can authenticate or verify every transaction in the block.

It takes the data from the transaction and verifies every detail and then reconciles it against its own ledger to ensure that the funds have not already been spent. If it receives any information that is incorrect, it will first reject the transaction and will cease all communication with you. This forces the node with incorrect information to be isolated and forced out of the system.

Mining

The process of verifying transactions and adding them to the Blockchain or the public ledger is called mining. This involves collecting all transactions and forming them into blocks and solving the mathematical codes. It's sort of a first come, first served basis. Any computer that solves the puzzle first gets to add the next block to the Blockchain and gets a reward for finding the solution.

Since every transaction takes place with an entire network of peers, everyone in the system has the same access to all transaction histories. Even if a database cannot be changed, everyone will still have access to every transaction in the entire network including the identities of each participant (encoded). Each record will also contain the buyer or seller's private keys, which contain all the confirmations of each transaction.

When a new transaction is established, it is automatically entered into the system, and once all the confirmation processes are verified, every single peer on the network will receive it.

If no confirmation is done, the request never moves beyond the initial stage and can be canceled. However, once they have been confirmed, it is added to the Blockchain; from then on, it is impossible to alter. The miner's job is to confirm all those transactions within the network.

Anyone with the right hardware can enter the system as a peer and become a miner.

Chapter 5: Investment

There are many ways you can make money using cryptocurrency. These digital currencies are becoming more and more popular with time, and the options for profit are many. Depending on your preference, you can choose to buy or sell them, become a miner, or offer a product or service for them over dedicated platforms.

Whatever you choose to do, there are several applications that can be used to help you first find the type of cryptocurrency you want to invest in and then make your investment. But before you even think about that, you must take some time to learn how to convert your traditional money into a digital currency.

Cryptocurrency Exchange Platform

Just like when exchanging traditional currency, digital currencies have exchange houses where they can be traded. These exchange houses usually work in a similar way to a financial institution where you can save your money, trade, offer, or receive loans.

These exchange houses are important as they will usually be the first and last stop whenever you're dealing with cryptocurrencies. Keep in mind that these exchange houses are not limited to only one type of currency but can offer several different ones. This is very helpful because you could buy and trade in one currency and then switch to another currency whenever you feel like it.

As these exchange houses play such an important role in your investment strategy, it is necessary to make sure you choose one carefully. This decision isn't just a matter of finding the house with the best transaction fees or how many different types of payments they accept, but you must also investigate the different types of cryptocurrencies they offer and find those that are most likely to match up with your investment goals.

When choosing digital currencies, the most commonly traded is the Bitcoin, so as a beginning investor, it is probably smart to start with a proven success. It is easy to find an exchange house that will accommodate them as opposed to those that are less popular. It may take you a while to find a house that can accommodate those less recognized in the cryptocurrency world.

Not only are Bitcoins commonly traded for many types of traditional currency, but they can be traded for other digital currencies as well. So, as you're investigating exchange houses, it will be helpful to understand the different trading pairs that each house is offering, so you know your options.

When it comes to service fees, while they may not be the most important factor in choosing an exchange house, they are definitely worth considering. Depending on the exchange house you choose, you could find yourself paying from a fraction of a percentage for each transaction to as much as 5% of your total earnings. However, there are also additional fees you need to factor into your choice of exchange houses. Many exchange houses will require a monthly service fee for housing your digital currency while others may demand an additional deposit or withdrawal fee.

These are fees that are most likely to get you into trouble when investing in cryptocurrency, so the more you familiarize yourself with these, the less likely you'll see your profits eaten away by these additional charges before you ever get to see any of it.

Always keep in mind that exchanges are not regulated like government-backed financial institutions. So, there is very little you can do if one of them folds and your money disappears. It is important that you do your due diligence and make sure of everything before you invest your money. Look for exchange houses that have a long-standing reputation and evaluate their security protocols before making any decisions. If you find a house with very little information about their track record, consider it as a warning that they may not have been around for very long and have no proof of staying power. It is better to take heed and move on.

The Cryptocurrency Wallet

No matter which cryptocurrency you want to invest in or which exchange house you use, you will have to set up a digital wallet. Many exchange houses offer you a wallet as part of their service, but others may require you to set up your own wallet by a third-party for storing your currency.

If you choose to go through a third-party storage facility, there are some good ones available to choose from. Wallets usually have a fixed rate that applies whether you're buying or selling. All you have to do is link your bank card or your bank account information to your wallet, and you're set up to make transactions.

There are pros and cons to investing in cryptocurrency in this way. First, on the positive side, you can make transactions very quickly and easily through the wallet.

You can liken it to making an online purchase with your credit or debit card; enter the necessary details, verify your identity, and you're done. You can even make these types of purchases through special ATMs that now offer cryptocurrencies. If you're more concerned about time, then this is one of the best ways to go.

However, you will also find that not all transaction pairs are offered this way. In many cases, getting your cryptocurrency exchanged for traditional funds may not always be easy. But a bigger issue to be concerned with is your risk of exposing your personal information and payment data. One of the reasons people choose to trade in cryptocurrency is because they want the anonymity that is offered in dealing with every transaction.

Peer-to-Peer

Another way to obtain cryptocurrency is to buy it from your peers. If you know someone who owns the kind of currency you want, you can simply buy directly from them. In fact, there are exchange houses that are set up simply to connect private buyers and sellers to each other. You can also find someone to trade with through online community forums.

If you don't have a personal network of traders set up, you can check with your wallet provider or online for local and private trading tools already built into the system. With these tools, you can find sellers living right in your immediate area that you can meet with and negotiate a trade.

It is important, however, if you choose to go this route to then verify the seller's reputation through testimonials, online checks, or whatever means necessary to ensure that they are legitimate. Remember, there is little recourse if you are taken in a scam, so make sure you find someone you can trust before you agree to anything.

Finally, if you choose to buy and sell privately, make sure that you conduct your business in a public arena. It should go without saying that meeting strangers for the first time to do a monetary transaction does not come without risk. Being in a public place with lots of people around can be more of a protection than you might realize.

Credit Card

In today's world, you can use credit cards to buy just about anything, including cryptocurrency. There are loads of online payment systems that will allow you to buy cryptocurrency on credit.

While this method is very easy, caution is still warranted. As a matter of fact, until you have a solid, long-lasting, established relationship with anyone, it is always best to err on the side of caution to make sure that everything they do and every interaction you have with them is completely above board.

Most of these platforms will accept Visa and MasterCard, but there are others that are capable of accepting other credit cards as well.

Wire Purchase

You can also purchase via wire. There are some exchanges or private individuals that will accept a wire transfer as a form of payment. However, this is probably the less popular choice as these transactions can literally take days to complete.

Online Payment Systems

Purchasing cryptocurrency using alternative payment systems like PayPal or some other form of online payment can be just as easy as purchasing using your bank or credit card. With this option, it is easy to set up an account with just your email address then link your card or bank account to the system.

Once done, you can complete a transaction quickly and easily.

The only drawback to this system is the additional service fees in place. However, these fees can be viewed as a protection as they almost always come with some protocol in place to handle dispute resolution when things don't necessarily go as planned.

Buy with Cash

This is especially beneficial when you're purchasing your digital currency from a peer. You can pay with cash when you meet or use cash transferred from your digital wallet at the point of agreement. This is probably the fastest mode of payment when buying cryptocurrency.

As you can see, there are many options when it comes to taking the first step in investing in cryptocurrency. While all of these options are good, there is no system without its flaws. Make sure you do your homework and get background on anyone that you plan to do business with. In the beginning, you may be unsure of which avenue will work best for you, so you might want to try several different tools to make sure you find the one that will work best.

Before You Invest

Now that you know all of your options for buying you need to make sure you do everything in the right order. This will help you to avoid having to pay any additional fees or getting bogged down in unnecessary steps to get started. Most of these guidelines listed below are just plain common sense, but investing in digital currency can be exciting and when we get too excited about something we forget to dot the i's and cross the t's.

- Determine your budget: Investing in anything requires a starting capital, so do a little price shopping. Once you know how much money you can afford to invest, it will be easy to determine which currencies you can buy.

- Determine the currency: Next you want to decide which currency you want to buy. With so much available, it is best to start with the most commonly traded on the market. There are lots of online resources that can give you some background knowledge about each type of coin, its history, and its potential for future placement on the market.

- Choose your exchange: Once you know the currency then begin by choosing which exchange you want to trade in. This will be the platform from where you will start every transaction. While many exchanges offer a variety of digital currencies, they may not all have the same menu or the same prices. Research them thoroughly before you set up an account. Don't forget to investigate their fee schedule and their payment methods as well.

- Set up your wallet: If the exchange house you select comes with your own wallet, you can skip this step, but if you have to go outside to set up your wallet with a third-party, then you will have to investigate further. It is important to understand that not all wallets are created equal. You will find several different types of wallets, and you may discover that you need more than one.

Insurance

It is always best to err on the side of caution and insurance is one of the best ways to do that. Some exchange houses offer insurance coverage to protect your currency, or you can choose to work with third-party carriers, but be warned these may come at an additional cost.

Start Buying

Now it is time to start building up your crypto portfolio. As we discussed before, you can begin by buying and selling on the exchange, but you can also connect with other people or websites to purchase your currency. To make your purchase, all you need to do is give them your public key in your wallet so they can transfer the currency to your account.

Trade

Once you have collected enough cryptocurrency, you may decide that you want to trade it for another type of currency. Once all the steps are done, you can easily make a trade through your exchange house or any exchange house that is set-up to exchange currencies for your particular pair.

No matter the choices you make, it is always important to ask a lot of questions before you make a final decision to invest. Remember, you will be dealing with assets that are not physical, so you won't walk away with something in your hand.

It's not like negotiating for a car where at the end of the process you can drive it off the lot. Everything will always remain in the digital realm, so you need to verify everything and then double check it to make sure you're getting what you're paying for.

When looking at a currency, you want to find something that will not only give you a good trade now but has the potential for generating earnings in the future.

Look for currencies that have the credibility and the history to show that you will be able to hold onto your money.

Make sure that the currency you choose is not going to drop in value overnight.

It is normal for a price to fluctuate up and down over time, but a currency that makes drastic drops is something to be wary of.

Ask yourself if you plan to be in this for the long haul or are you looking for short-term returns. Once you're set up, it is just as easy to exit a trade as it is to get into it. However, in determining how long you will stay will depend on what type of market you want to play in. A bullish market is more favorable to buyers, a bearish market is more favorable to sellers, and a break-even market is just what it says it is.

Beginners usually rely on several basic strategies until they get comfortable with the market. They may start with something as simple as arbitrage where transactions are made very quickly. You buy low and sell high. Since there are no standard market rates to go by, you can buy from one market and sell the same day to another market and make a profit as you do.

It's about seeking out and exploiting the opportunities you find. It's an easy way to earn a profit but be wary of the fees, or you may find yourself losing money in the process.

Another strategy that beginners often use is short-term trading. In these cases, investors buy currency as the price is slowly inching up and then hold onto it watching as the price moves beyond what was paid for it. Then they sell it making a tidy little profit along the way. The entire transaction can be done in a matter of hours or days. Doing this on a regular basis could bring in a steady income if you keep your eye out for the right margin.

The Top Cryptocurrencies to Invest in 2017

While the decision on which currency you choose will always lie with you, experts have made several recommendations for the currencies that show the best potential for 2017.

Bitcoin:

As always, Bitcoin is leading the pack as the currency with the most potential. With a market cap at over $75 billion, you can buy one Bitcoin at a little more than $3,600 (as of September 2017). This makes it the most expensive of cryptocurrencies on the market today.

If you're not ready to put that much down on a single Bitcoin, you can start by a Satoshi (the smallest fraction of a Bitcoin). It is the equivalent of 000,000,001 of a full Bitcoin. That means that if you buy 1 Bitcoin at $3,641, a single Satoshi can cost you only $0.00004019, which amounts to only a fraction of a cent in USD.

Ethereum

Today's market cap for Ethereum is nearly $31 million with a price of about $328 for a single coin.

Ethereum has been steadily growing month by month increasing its potential for profit as it does so. It has a proven track record that allows its team of developers to solve issues on a real-time basis.

Monero

Monero is gaining popularity because of its perfect world of anonymity. Because they go to great lengths to keep the identity of the investor private, many people are flocking to it. This is unlike other cryptocurrencies that maintain anonymity where once you give your wallet address to anyone they can see all of the transactions you have made in the past. While they cannot see the identity of who you traded with without decoding the information, it is clear that your secrecy is only as strong as your code.

With Monero, it is different. Its software is designed to mix your coins with other investor's coins, so you have no idea who owns what or how much. The market cap for Monero is approximately 1/100th of a Bitcoin, which makes it a much more affordable investment in the long run.

Ripple

Ripple has become more popular mainly because its software allows transactions to be conducted almost instantaneously. It also drastically reduces the cost of transaction fees making it extremely favorable for the investor. It is believed that Ripple will exceed the market capitalization of Bitcoin by March 2018 at the latest.

CRYPTOCURRENCY

Ripple has been accepted by over 70 (and counting) banks, some of them are definitively big names (UBS, BoA, BBVA, NBAD...)

Should You Invest in Cryptocurrency?

Cryptocurrency is a very new and innovative system that is appealing in many ways for an investor. There are several reasons why people are now taking a closer look at investing in cryptocurrency.

1. Security: While there is no such thing as 100% security in dealing with cryptocurrency, these coins are considered to be a much safer investment than housing traditional money.

2. Value: Aside from the security, when any asset you invest in has the potential to see a 30% increase in the value of the course of just a few weeks, it is certainly going to attract the attention of many people.

3. Autonomy: As it is not backed by any government or organization, its autonomy doesn't allow it to be controlled by geographical limitations, financial preferences, or political entities.

4. Decentralized: Finally, the fact that the investments are not held on a centralized server makes it much more difficult for hackers to access to it and compromise the system. Its value, therefore, is based more on supply and demand rather than by some third-party management system.

Chapter 6: Mining

If you've read anything about cryptocurrency, you've heard the term "mining" repeated quite often. While you may have a pretty good idea of what mining is in the physical sense, you may be a little confused about its role in the world of digital currencies.

Now let's get a little deeper into how cryptocurrency transactions are done. A crucial part of this process is what is called mining. While the process happens with all digital currencies, we'll use the Bitcoin as our primary example as we explain this rather complicated process.

What Is Cryptocurrency Mining?

With traditional currency, its value is determined or backed by the government that issued it, however, with cryptocurrency, there is no governmental backing, so how is the value determined? Essentially, it comes from a complicated series of mathematical computations referred to as "mining." The purpose of these calculations is twofold,

1) It confirms the transactions.

2) It keeps the network security intact.

One of the great things about mining cryptocurrency is the monetary rewards you can gain. Imagine being able to earn thousands of Bitcoins simply by running a program on your computer.

This is one of the key reasons why this system has become wildly successful. As a miner, for each new coin you discover as your computer trolls through the system, you will be rewarded. It is a highly popular way to earn money and support the system at the same time. Also, miners collect transaction fees each time they add a block to the Blockchain.

However, to do this, you must have the right hardware on hand. If you hope to become a cryptocurrency miner, then you will have to have more than just a simple computer to get the job done. Here is what you'll need:

● CPU

The CPU or the Central Processing Unit is the key component in your computer that handles the everyday processes that your system needs. Its primary purpose is to make the big decisions for your computer's functions. It is comprised of the electronic circuitry and performs all the functions of a computer program. While in the beginning, this was the only way to mine for currency, it was not the most efficient.

While the CPU is no longer the primary way to mine cryptocurrency, it is still used to earn a little money on the network. Many miners will use their CPU to join a mining pool. By doing this, they can combine their computing power with others to earn money. The potential for earning will still be limited, but if you're just interested in a few earnings, you can definitely garner a little cash this way.

● GPU

The GPU of a computer is responsible for the real heavy lifting a computer does. It manages the graphics processing and does all the complex mathematical computations involved in running videos. It is much faster than CPU mining and is considerably more powerful.

Many miners may have a system that maintains multiple GPU units to get the most power and speed possible.

● FPGA

The Field Programmable Gate Array is a piece of hardware that is solely dedicated to mining. It is considered to be the next level of mining as it has increased the speed and efficiency of mining many times over. A bonus of setting up your mining platform using the FPGA is that it draws very little power and you can keep it running 24-hours a day earning your profit around the clock.

- ASIC

The last in a long line of mining technology is the ASIC (Application Specific Integrated Circuit) chips. First introduced in 2013, they have been steadily improving with each passing year. Like the FPGA, they have only one job, and that is to mine 24/7.

When it comes to mining, speed is extremely important, and with new hardware like the FPGA and the ASIC, older and slower systems will never be able to compete. While you can still mine with CPUs and GPUs, your potential for profit in the world of mining will depend largely on how fast your computer can troll the network for those transactions.

Getting set up to mine for cryptocurrency doesn't have to be hard. Before you can do that, however, you need to decide if you're going to be a lone miner or join a pool. Depending on which avenue you choose to take you'll have to set up your mining business differently.

Let us start with the individual miner and how to get set up.

1. Set up your own virtual private server (VPS) to perform the mining. This should be set aside to only use for your mining operations.

2. Access your VPS.

3. Follow the commands to set up the system to start mining.

4. Start mining.

It is important to know that the energy required to mine can be quite extensive, so many choose to join mining pools. While you won't make as much money as you would individually, you'll save on energy in the process.

You also have the option of installing specialized mining software that can run on your local machine and it can be run on as many servers as you want to speed up the process.

Once you're registered on your server, all you need is your email address you used to sign up and then follow the commands. When all of that is in place, you're ready to start mining and make money.

One of the challenges for individual miners is the difficulty in finding those blocks. For some, it was years before they were able to generate a block and earn a piece of the pie, so joining a pool is much more practical for those who don't mind sharing the reward. It will require a smaller investment but increase the rewards exponentially. You will earn an income on a more regular basis.

Getting paid for mining can also be a little confusing to work out. You have several options to choose from.

PPS (Pay per Share): This option gives you instant payouts for every share of the block that your system solves. The money is taken out of pool's balance and can be withdrawn immediately.

PROP (Proportional pay): This payment method divides up the rewards based on the number of shares each miner has found in the pool and paid it out proportionately.

BPM or the Slush Pool: This type of pool divides the reward based on who participated towards the end of a block rather than those who participated throughout.

There are several other methods of divvying up and paying out when you are a part of a pool. To get a better understanding of it and to help you find out which one works best for you, it is strongly suggested that you get the details from each pool before you join.

How Does Cryptocurrency Mining Work?

To understand mining, one must begin with understanding the Blockchain and how it works. When you think of a Blockchain, it is best to try to visualize it as a public ledger that is constantly being updated every second. It is not under any central control, but as each transaction is completed, it is added to the ledger, keeping a running total of everything that is happening with that particular cryptocurrency. The miner's job is to find those Bitcoins, validate each transaction and record every completed transaction as a new block on the Blockchain.

To accomplish this, miners need to have the power to search these out.

How to Mine Your Cryptocurrency

Okay, now let's look at exactly how to find those blocks to add to the chain.

There are several steps involved in the mining process.

1. Spending: When a user decides he wants to buy goods from another user he will use his wallet to send 1 Bitcoin to the seller.

1. Announcement: An announcement that 1 Bitcoin payment needs to go to the seller's wallet is broadcast to all the nodes or computers connected to the buyer's wallet.

1. Propagation: The nodes then look at the buyer's spend amount and compares it to any other transactions that may still be pending. If they find no conflicts, the nodes broadcast the transaction to the entire network.

1. Miners will take their copy of the Blockchain and monitor for any new transactions that may be coming. It then works to fit all new and verified transactions into the block.

The miner who completes the work faster and provides its work test (the hash) actually receives the reward.

Every solved block receives a substantial reward.

1. Confirmation: The miner solves the block and it announces it to the network. If the other nodes are in agreement, the new block is added to the Blockchain, and the miner starts again looking for a new problem to solve.

1. Notification: The seller is notified and can now send his product to the buyer secure in knowing that the funds have been transferred successfully.

This process is pretty straightforward, but in some cases, it can become quite complicated. Especially in situations where large sums of money are being transferred and where more than one confirmation may be necessary to ensure the validity of the transaction.

Chapter 7: How to Store and Secure Cryptocurrency

Even though cryptocurrency is digital in format, it still needs to be stored in a safe place. When you have physical money, you usually can keep it in your wallet or open an account at the bank. For those with a lot of money on hand, a safe or another form of storage may be necessary.

When it comes to cryptocurrency, storage decisions may not be so simple.

Every transaction made with cryptocurrency is kept on a Blockchain, which holds a number of wallets that are provided for account holders. But it is best to avoid thinking of these wallets in the same way you might think of a safe deposit box or a safe in a bank.

The wallet you have access to will have two addresses. The first address is a public one. This address or key is needed so that others can send you money when you sell. The private address is password protected and will give you access to your funds when you want to make a withdrawal or a deposit. The private key is also used to transfer funds to other account holders.

It is important to protect your private key above all else. View it like you would view any other important documents (social security number, passport number, etc.) It should never be revealed to anyone unless you want to give them access to your money.

Online wallet: The standard wallet for digital currency is the online wallet that you can easily access through your browser. It is strongly recommended that you do not put all your currency in your online wallet.

One of the reasons for this is because they become very tempting targets for hackers who will spend a lot of energy trying to break their codes and get into them.

Online wallets are usually the fastest way to complete any transaction, they are perfect for holding small sums of currency, and some can hold more than one currency at a time allowing you to transfer your money from one to the next.

However, they are often the target of phishing scams, malware, hacking, and other means criminals might use to get around your security measures. They often defeat the purpose of investing in cryptocurrency (to cut out the middleman) as they store information with a third-party.

Mobile Wallet: Mobile wallets are great for people who are constantly on the move. These work well from mobile devices, so wherever you can get access to the Internet, you can make your transactions.

They tend to be more practical and convenient to use, and most can accept or send payments quickly. Some even can produce a QR code that can be scanned to complete a transaction.

Caution, however, is warranted because your smartphone is likely the least secure device in your arsenal. Phones can be compromised very easily, and even encryption software is not safe if your phone has been exposed to malware, keyloggers, or web viruses.

Desktop Wallet: Considered to be the safest of all wallets, desktop wallets have several advantages. They are probably the easiest to use and work as the ideal "cold storage" solution to housing your cryptocurrency. Cold storage simply means housing your keys offline where Internet hackers cannot get to it.

While it is considered to be the safest, desktop wallets are only as safe as the computer and Internet service you use. Without the proper security measures in place, your computer can be just as exposed as with any other type of wallet. Also, you must always remember to backup your computer because if for some reason it fails, your access to your currency dies with it.

Hardware Wallet: These are not as user-friendly as other wallets, but they are easy to use and more secure than a hot wallet (a wallet kept online). It works in the same way as a paper wallet (listed below) where your currency is stored offline.

They have the same security as other wallets, but are only vulnerable to criminal activity when connected online.

Hardware wallets have two parts; one that is connected to the Internet and the other that is not. The part that is connected to the Internet houses the public keys and performs all of the same functions as other wallets, however, it does not have access to the private key, so it cannot sign off on any transactions.

When you are ready to begin a transaction, you connect the offline device via a USB port or scan it in with a QR code to authorize and complete the transaction.

While it does have some vulnerabilities, it is considered to be the most secure way to store your cryptocurrency on a long-term basis. Still, it can be very tedious to use, but is one of the most important tools to have when transferring large quantities of cryptocurrencies.

Paper Wallet: A great way to safely manage your cryptocurrency as it is an offline tool for storing your digital currency. A paper wallet allows you to print out your private keys and address onto physical paper. Depending on what security measures you have in place it can be one of the safest ways to avoid your currency being stolen by an outside hacker.

None of your keys are entered into the computer until you are ready to use them, and nothing is stored on a third-party server making it one of the safest ways to store your currency. It does, however, require much more work to trade currencies or move them around and it is more technical to grasp how to use it fully.

When choosing the right wallet, there are several things you need to keep in mind. Each wallet has its own pros and cons, so it is important to consider your personal needs when you choose. Here are just a few factors you might want to consider

1. Convenience: Make sure that the wallet will be convenient for you to use when you need it. Choose something that will work with several different types of cryptocurrencies but also is compatible with some different software programs and exchange platforms.

1. Accessibility: You need to able to get to your coins when you need them. Make sure access is 24/7.

1. Security: Know the security protocols for your wallet. Check its history and look for any instances of hacking and what was done about it.

1. Utility: Your wallet should be user-friendly. Mistakes can be extremely costly when dealing with cryptocurrencies, and once transactions have been validated, there is no turning back.

1. Cost: Investors always look for transaction fees when they are thinking about cryptocurrency, but you must also factor in the cost of storing your currency.

There are many free wallets available with no cost,s but those wallets generally give you limited functions, so if you want to do more complex forms of trade, it is a good idea to find one with a monthly fee.

Since there is a variety of wallet options to choose from, it should not be difficult to find the one that will work best for your circumstances. Just keep in mind that every wallet has its own pros and cons, so make sure you factor all of that in before making a decision.

Chapter 8: Mistakes to Avoid While Trading Cryptocurrencies

There are many people now who are learning about cryptocurrencies and are ready to trade. However, as with all types of investments, getting too emotionally involved or too excited about the venture can lead to trouble. You forget to take the necessary precautions, and you usually end up losing out in the end. Newcomers to the digital currency trade tend to make the same types of mistakes and end up in situations that they could have easily avoided if they had been forewarned.

Here are the most common mistakes you should try to avoid when you start trading in the cryptocurrency market.

Weakly informed

No matter what your goals are or what you expect to get out of your investment strategy, knowledge can be your best friend, or it can be your worst enemy if you don't have it. It pays to do a lot of research before deciding to jump into the deep end. As you can see from what we've discussed already, it can be very easy to make money with cryptocurrency, but it can be very costly if you make a mistake.

Just the fact that once a block is set up on the Blockchain it cannot be reversed or altered should be warning enough that mistakes can be extremely costly. People have lost thousands of dollars simply by inputting the wrong information, giving their code to the wrong people, or just not doing their homework and investing in the wrong type of currency.

Before you invest, always learn as much as you can about the currency, the protocols, the security in place, the fees, and anything else that may affect your return on investment. Learn the history of the currency, the exchange, the activity, and always have a plan in place before you start.

Without regulatory conditions in place, you are solely responsible for what happens to your money. If you don't fully understand it or you're just making a decision based on what other people tell you, trouble is definitely waiting for you down the line.

Investing Without a Plan

This applies to any type of investment tool you plan to use, but it is even more important when dealing with cryptocurrency. Before you ever put a dollar into the market, you must have a strategy for how you're going to get it out.

Set rules for yourself that will help to remove the emotion from the trade. You should already have in mind under what conditions you plan to sell and the terms for when you need to get out of the market to cut your losses. Once you've started down that road to investing, decide what strategies you will take to improve your performance and your return on investment.

Use the history and data you found during your research to create a solid plan of action so that you're not caught later on having a knee-jerk reaction to a sudden change in the market.

Buying into Scams

There are many opportunities available when you're dealing with cryptocurrency, but there are also many opportunities to lose everything if you're not careful.

New traders are often duped because they lack the experience or knowledge needed to distinguish between a legitimate trade and someone who is trying to pull the wool over their eyes.

In the beginning, try to avoid investing in new and unproven coins that have been "recently developed" and wait until they have established a solid reputation in the market.

Even when trading with well-known coins, look to purchase them at the lowest price possible from reputable exchange houses. It might be even better to wait until you are sure before you jump in. The wait may reduce your chances of a bigger profit, but it can also save you from buying a currency that has no profitability.

Leaving the Coins Un-exchanged

Leaving your coins on the exchange is tantamount to expecting someone else to take care of your money. You might think that leaving your money in the exchange is the same as depositing it in the bank, but there is a huge difference.

When you deposit money in the bank, your account is FDIC insured, but with cryptocurrency, there is no such protection. Every day, hackers, scammers, and all sorts of people are trying to break the system.

Once you've made your investment and secured your profits, you should immediately transfer those funds to your private wallet (preferably maintained offline), which is protected by your private key. This way, only you and those you authorize have access to it.

Choosing the Wrong Exchange

All exchanges are not created equal, so it's important that you make your trades with an exchange designed to suit your purposes. This is also why it's good to conduct thorough research and have a plan before you invest. Some exchanges have a solid reputation and can be trusted while others may have a questionable history.

Choosing the wrong exchange can cause anything from problems getting your money out when you want it to not having access to it at all.

Having Your Finger in Too Many Pies

With so many currencies to choose from, it could be very tempting to dab a little here and try a little there hoping to hit the big time. But when you are trading too many altcoins at one time it can have a negative effect on your portfolio. For newcomers, it is best to start off with one or two currencies and then as you gain experience diversify more as you learn how to evaluate the risks.

These are not the only things you should be wary of when you invest in cryptocurrency. Consider this list as just a start. There are many things you need to be watchful of, and as you learn the system, you'll soon learn how to identify various danger signs that could spell a trap where your money could fall through and end up out of your reach.

Even the most experienced of traders make mistakes from time to time, but the newcomer is especially vulnerable. Do your research and ask a lot of questions and you'll not only find the most profitable trades, but you'll also find you are more confident in your decisions, which could reduce the risk of impulsive and emotional trading that can be the cause of the trouble.

The Pros and Cons of Cryptocurrency

A cryptocurrency is a unique form of currency. Its ability to use encryption techniques to encode transactions sets it apart from any other currency we have ever used in the past. As it grows in popularity, more and more people are becoming fascinated by this new innovation, and it is enticing people from all over the globe to get in on its high potential for profit.

When you speak with those who trade in this currency, it is likely that you hear many positive things about it. At the same time, you might hear many raise questions and doubts about its legitimacy. Like all other currencies, many good things can be said about it, but it is not all that glitz and glam either. There are many valid and legitimate claims that present genuine risks as well.

The Pros

There are many good things that we can list here, but we'll try to keep the list down to a reasonable size.

Transparency: When trading in digital currency, all transactions are recorded and monitored. When a transaction has been completed, it is added to the ledger, and it becomes a permanent part of the record. This information cannot be manipulated or altered in any way. No individual or organization can change it, making it one of the most secure of all transactions.

Since assets can be moved securely from one user to another, it significantly reduces the risk of fraud or tampering by outside parties.

Global Reach: No matter where you are in the world, if you have access to the Internet you can trade in cryptocurrency, but because it is not backed by any geographical boundaries or governmental institutions, it is accepted and used in most countries of the world. That cannot be said about any other traditional currency in the world.

Low Transaction Fees: The fact that the transaction fees for trading in cryptocurrency are a mere fraction of the fees that most financial institutions charge makes it extremely appealing. The larger the transaction, the more you'll benefit from this as it can save you hundreds upon thousands of dollars.

You Control Your Money: Void of any middleman or third-party interests, no one is in charge of your money but you.

Cons

Lack of Acceptance: One of the biggest negatives with cryptocurrencies is their newness. While users can do a lot of things with them; buy, sell, trade, or purchase, it is not like the whole world would accept them like they do VISA or American Express. Finding vendors that are willing to accep crypto for the payment of goods and services is not always easy. Until it is, users will have to exchange their currency for local currency to make most purchases.

Volatile: While Bitcoin is a pretty stable currency, most other cryptocurrencies are not. When you are ready to invest, it is important to remember that it should be treated more like a commodity. Prices can fluctuate wildly depending on the flow of the market. If you view it more as a long-term investment, then you won't be sidetracked by the constant price fluctuations.

Cannot be Recovered if Lost: We've said it several times throughout the pages of this book. Cryptocurrencies cannot be recovered if they are lost. Unlike financial institutions that have regulations to protect your investment, a single incident of hacking could literally wipe you out. For that reason, keeping your currency off the Internet when not in an active trade is the best way to protect your investment.

Still in Development: Cryptocurrency is a baby on the world's economic scene, and while it has a very promising future, it is very important that you keep it in perspective. It is still in development, and there will likely be many changes coming in the future. Investors must be prepared to accept and adapt to these changes before the system is fully perfected.

Conclusion: Ways to Make Money with Cryptocurrency

For years, many people have been interested in investing in the stock market, mutual funds, Federal Bonds, IRAs, and all sorts of investment tools. In many cases, they have been prevented because the capital to get into these instruments is often out of reach for the average person. This keeps the profit potential squarely in the hands of the wealthy with only a few others getting in on the privilege.

All of that changes when you're looking at making money with cryptocurrency. One would be very surprised at what one can do with just a small investment of a few dollars. Without expensive broker fees, commission paid to middlemen, and no minimum investment requirement, even the average Joe will be able to turn a few dollars in short order. Here are just a few ways you can make money using cryptocurrency.

Bitcoin Trading

Probably the easiest way to make money is by trading Bitcoin. With Bitcoin, you can trade with every other cryptocurrency on the market. All you need to do is buy the Bitcoin, scour the market for a better price and then sell it again.

When trading with other currencies, always make sure you're trading for a currency you can sell later. When the price reaches a point where you can turn a profit, simply sell it and reap the rewards

Lending - Loan some Bitcoins, earn some interest

Interest rates will vary with the risk involved. If you get collateral in exchange for your loan, interest rates will be low. No collateral means higher risks, but it also means higher interest rates.

Peer to peer lending

You can also do peer-to-peer lending online. You can literally become your own bank and choose who you'd like to invest your money in. With Smart Contracts, you can even set your own terms and conditions for the loans and then receive regular payments from your benefactor with interest.

Selling products and services.

If you already have a business, you can sell your products or services online and accept Bitcoin or another cryptocurrency as payment.

Investing

Many people new to the market choose to buy Bitcoin and hold onto it for the long term. While the price fluctuates greatly from day to day, the overall trend has been consistently on the rise. The longer you hold onto it, the better your chances of a larger return on your investment.

Cloud Mining

CRYPTOCURRENCY

Mining Bitcoin is a very active way to make money with cryptocurrency. With the right hardware and the time, you can generate a steady stream of income over an extended period of time.

Just because you have finished reading this book doesn't mean that it stops here. You are required to expand your horizons if you want to learn more about cryptocurrency. When done, stop reading and think about how you can implement the things you have discovered in real life and improve your living standard.